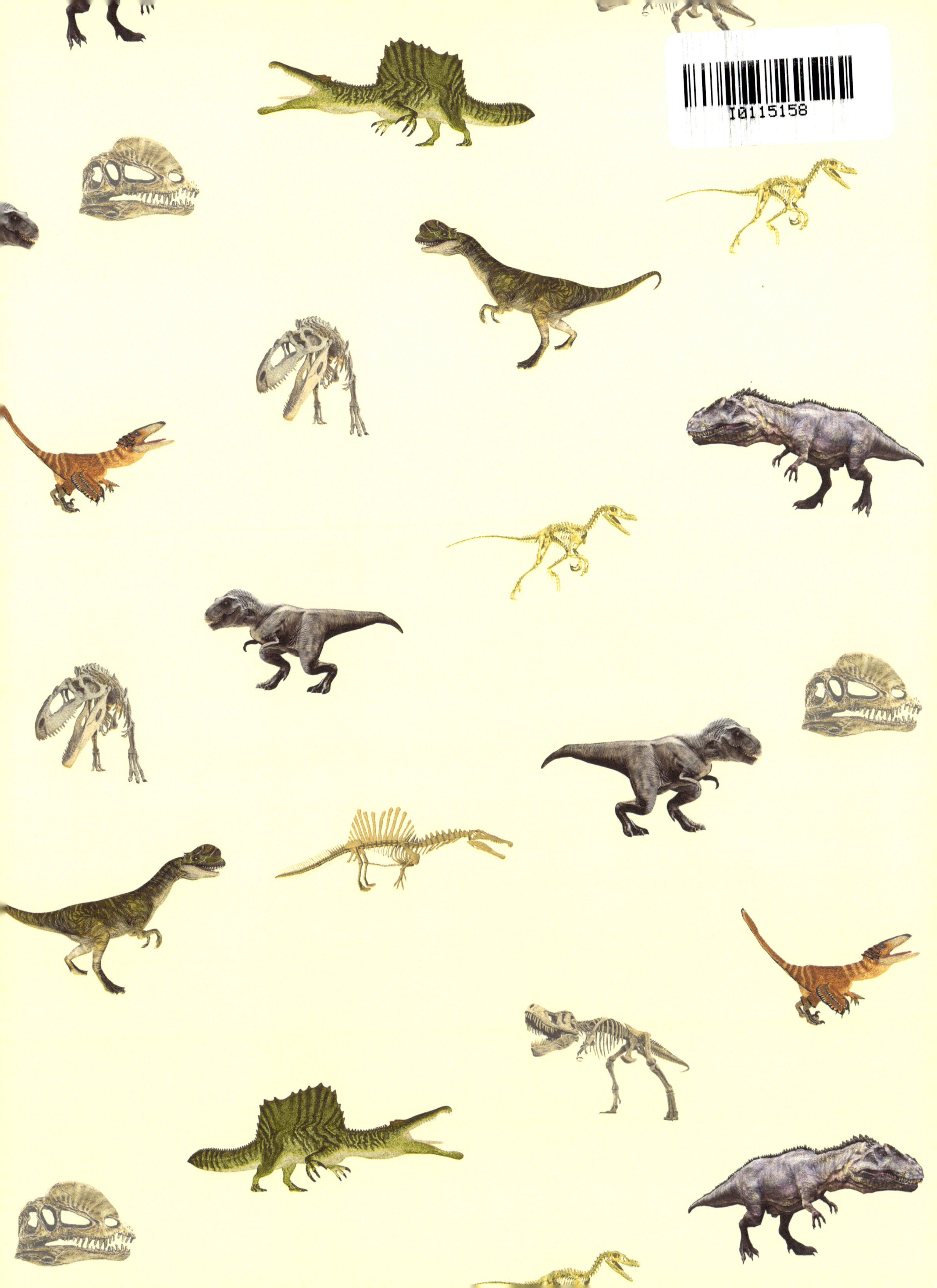

MEET THE T-REX FAMILY

See dinosaurs in real

By Sasa Minimuthu

This book belongs to:

_____

SEE DINOSAURS IN REAL

All dinosaurs in this book can be viewed in 3D and placed in your real environment using Augmented reality. They will appear in their real size.

You can place all of them together to create your own Dinosaur park.

STEP 1
Scan QR code next to each dinosaur.

STEP 2
View dinosaur in 3D and click the heart icon (♡) at the top left corner.
Click the eye icon (👁) to open your dinosaur collection.

Click to add to collection •

Open collection •

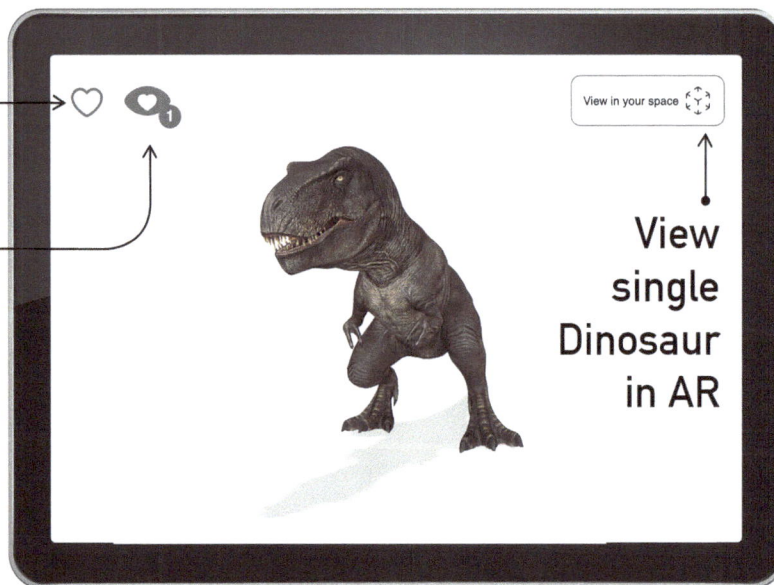

View in your space

View single Dinosaur in AR

STEP 3

View all dinosaurs in your real environment using Augmented reality.
You can place any number of dinosaurs to create your own dinosaur park.

TYRANNOSAURUS REX

" KING OF THE TYRANT LIZARDS"

(tai.ra.nuh.saw.ruhs-reks)

T.rex ruled the cretaceous. It was the most powerful land predator ever and no animal was a match for it.

I AM THE KING OF THE

POWERFUL TAIL
The tail balances the heavy body

POWERFUL LEGS
The legs had huge thigh muscles for changing into the attack with lethal speed

When: 67-66 MYA   **Where:** North America   **Period:** Late Cretaceous   **Habitat:** Forest and swamp

DINOSAURS

SMALL TWO FINGER ARMS

Scientists aren't sure why T. rex had such little arms

TERRIFYING TEETH

Its sharp pointed teeth were strong enough to crunch through the heavy armor of its prey. When teeth are broken, new ones grow to replace them

Lenght: 12 m   **Height:** 5 m   **Weight:** 5,000-7,000 Kg   **Diet:** Large dinosaurs

TYRANNOSAURUS REX
SKELETON

24 rib bones

35 tail vertebrae

Hip Bone

Leg Bones

Scientists found my 90 % complete skeleton

Triassic Period	Jurassic Period	Cretaceous Period
251 Million Years Ago	200 Million Years Ago	145 Million Years Ago

Mesozoic Era

Large wide eyes socket
Provided exceptional depth perception and was capable to see long distances

Nose hole

Skull holes were used to cool their heads

60 serrated teeth, Each is about eight inches long

Short arms with two-fingered hand

Scientists have found most T-Rex fossils in the Northwest of Northern America, in states such as Montana and South Dakota. T-Rex fossils have also been found in Alberta, and Canada.

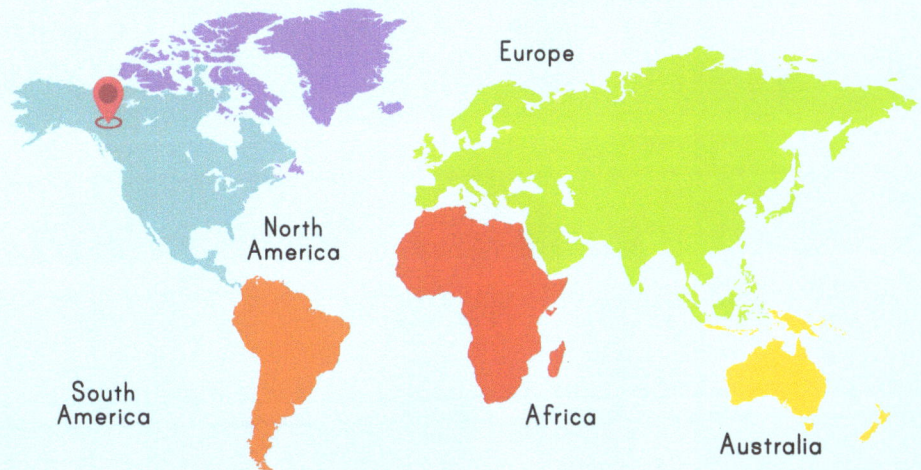

Europe

North America

South America

Africa

Australia

Large *Tyrannosaurus* compared with a 1.8 meter tall person.

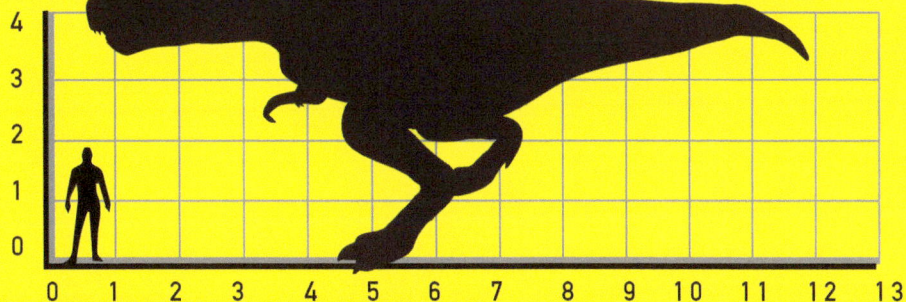

4
3
2
1
0

0 1 2 3 4 5 6 7 8 9 10 11 12 13

GIGANOTOSAURUS

"GIANT SOUTHERN LIZARD"

(jiga-note-a saw-us)

There's a giant on the prowl and this giant a predator might have been even bigger than the legendary T rex.

FORMIDABLE WEAPONS TEETH

It had 8 inches of serrated, knife-like teeth

Short arms with three fingers

When: 99.6-97 MYA   **Where:** Argentina   **Period:** Cretaceous

I AM THE LARGEST TERRESTRIAL CARNIVORES EVER TO HAVE WALKED THE EARTH

POINTED TAIL
Which may have provided balance and the ability to make quick turns while running

Powerful legs

Length: 12 - 13 m   **Height:** 3.5 - 4 m   **Weight:** 4,200-14,000 Kg   **Diet:** Large dinosaurs

GIGANOTOSAURUS
SKELETON

Eye socket

Skull hole

Nose hole

Same flat, serrated teeth. Giganotosaurus had 76 teeth, and each tooth was eight inches long.

Triassic Period	Jurassic Period	Cretaceous Period
251 Million Years Ago	200 Million Years Ago	145 Million Years Ago

Mesozoic Era

Scientists found my 70% complete skeleton

Leg bones

Hip bone

Europe

North America

South America

Africa

Australia

Scientists have found most of Gifanotosauru's fossils in Argentina.

Large *Giganotosaurus* compared with a 1.8 meter tall person.

SPINOSAURUS

"SPINE LIZARD"

spine-oh-sore-us

This is one of the most exciting dinosaurs ever discovered, but most mysterious because only a few of its bones have been found.

Straight cortical teeth

LONG AND FLEXIBLE NECK

The neck allowed Spinosaurus to strike fast with its specialized jaws.

When: 112-97 MYA   **Where:** North Africa   **Period:** Cretaceous   **Habitat:** Tropical swamp

I AM THE BIGGEST PREDATOR TO EVER WALK THE EARTH.

SPECTACULAR SAIL
The tall sail rising from the dinosaur's back made it look even bigger.

Three-fingered hands and big curved claws. It may be used to hook fish from the water.

WEBBED TOE
The toes were long and flat undersides to the claws.

Length: 16 m   **Height:** 5.4 m   **Weight:** 12,00-20,000 Kg   **Diet:** Fish

SPINOSAURUS
SKELETON

Skull holes helped regulate temperatures inside its head

Eye socket

Approximately 64 straight conical teeth

Scientists found Six main partial specimens of a Spinosaurus

Short arm with three-fingered hand

Triassic Period	Jurassic Period	Cretaceous Period
251 Million Years Ago	200 Million Years Ago	145 Million Years Ago

Mesozoic Era

Massive bony sail

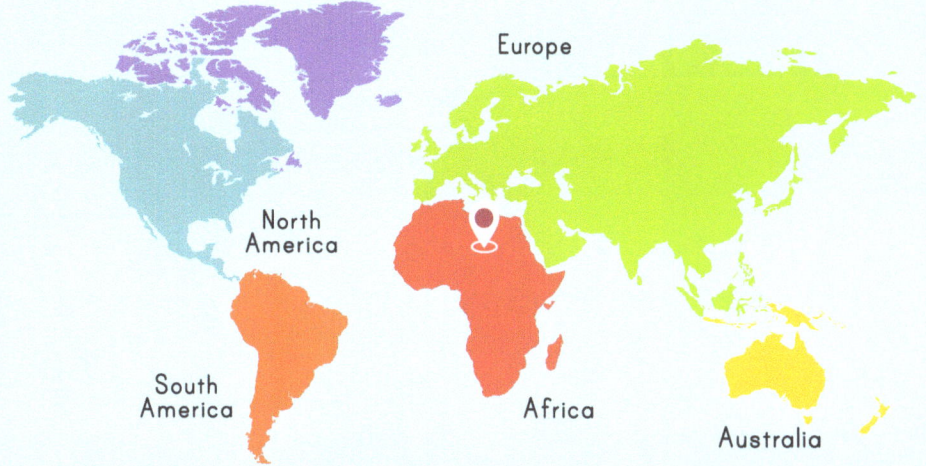

Scientists have found most Spinosaurus fossils in the North Africa

Europe

North America

South America

Africa

Australia

Unique, paddlelike tail.

Leg bones

Large Spinosaurus compared with a 1.8-meter tall person.

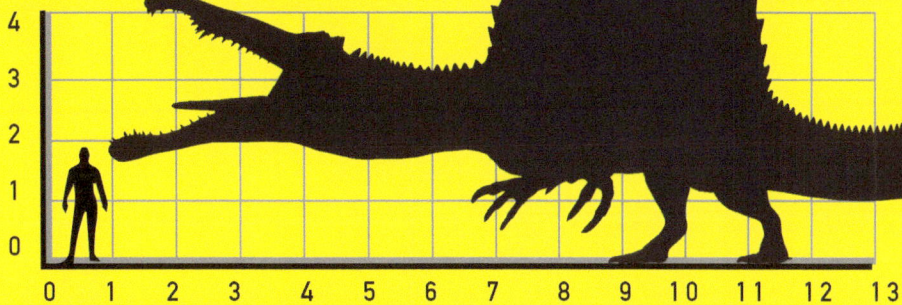

4
3
2
1
0

0 1 2 3 4 5 6 7 8 9 10 11 12 13

VELOCIRAPTOR

" SPEEDY THIEF "

vel -oss-ee-rap-tor

This feathered dinosaur used its clever brain along with its sharp weapons, killing claws, grasping hands, and needle-like teeth. It could bring down prey larger than itself.

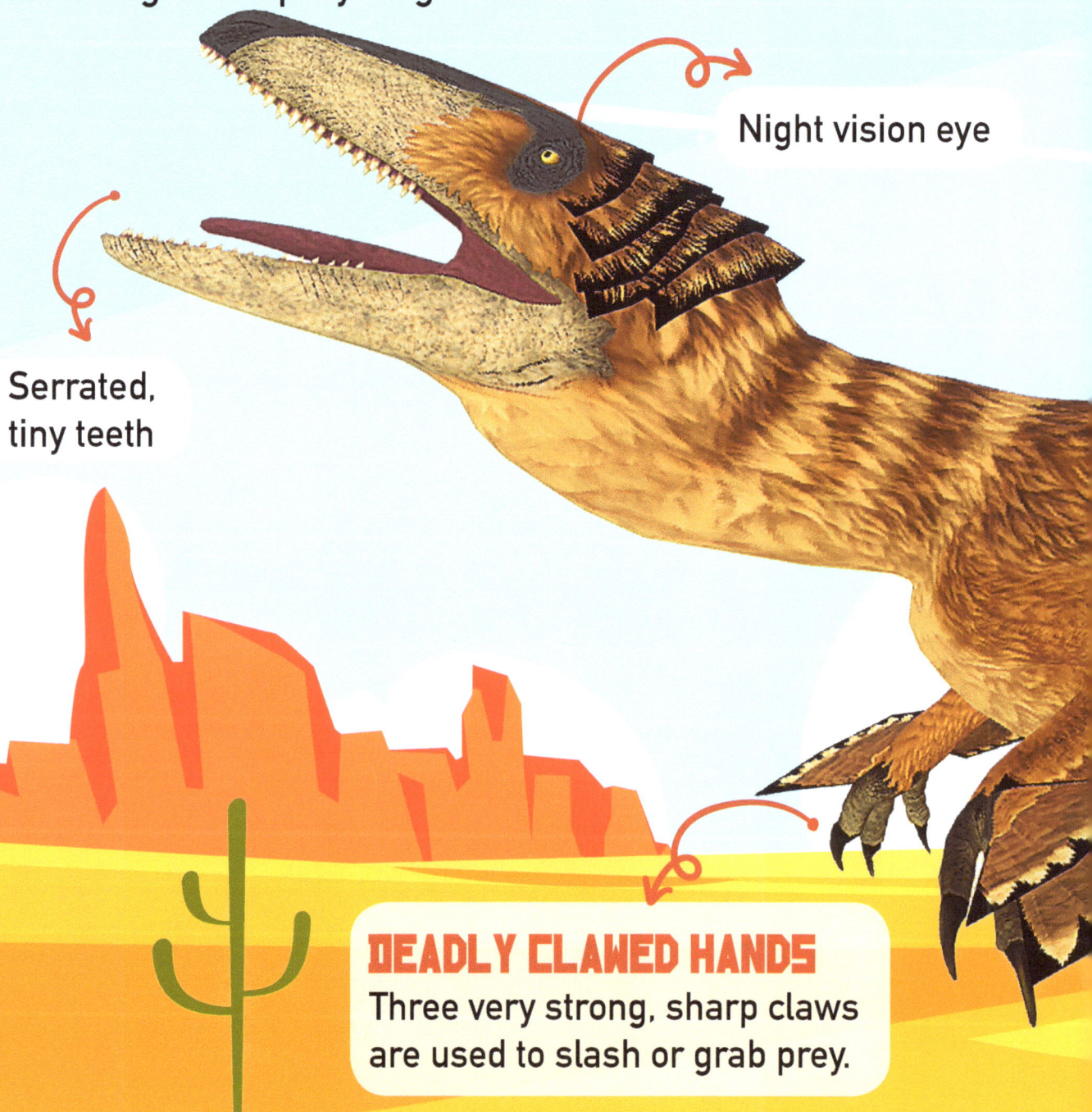

Night vision eye

Serrated, tiny teeth

DEADLY CLAWED HANDS
Three very strong, sharp claws are used to slash or grab prey.

When: 75-71 MYA   **Where:** Asia   **Period:** Late Cretaceous   **Habitat:** Scrubland and deserts

THE LONG AND BONY FEATHERED TAIL

It fringed with feathers just like the tails of the earliest birds.

FEATHERED ARMS

The arms covered long feathers for show off, and for covering eggs in the nest.

I AM SMALL ... BUT ONE OF THE MORE INTELLIGENT DINOSAURS.

SEE ME IN REAL

Length: 1.8 m   **Height:** 0.6 m   **Weight:** 45 Kg   **Diet:** Lizards, mammals and small dinosaurs

VELOCIRAPTOR
SKELETON

Fused tail bones

Leg bones

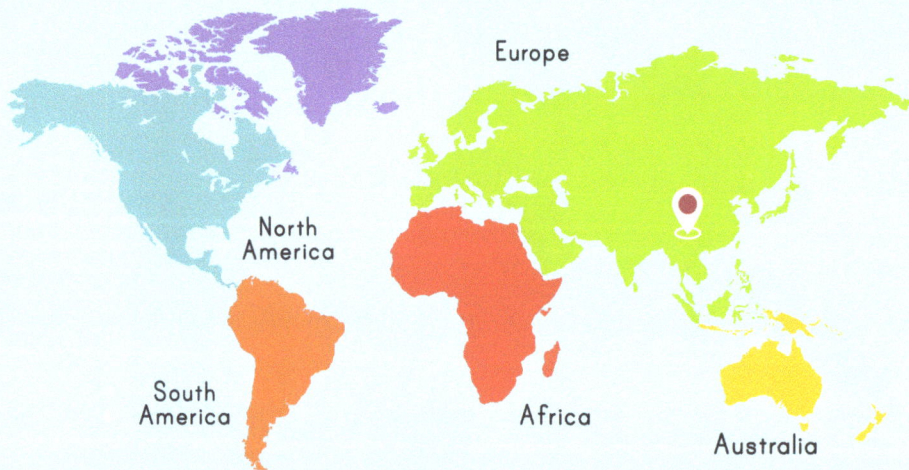

Scientists have found most Velociraptor fossils in northern China and Mongolia in the Gobi desert.

Triassic Period	Jurassic Period	Cretaceous Period
● 251 Million Years Ago	● 200 Million Years Ago	● 145 Million Years Ago

Mesozoic Era

Skull hole

Nose Hole

Eye Socket

Big curved claw

Hip bone

Scientists believe, I had between 70-100 bones

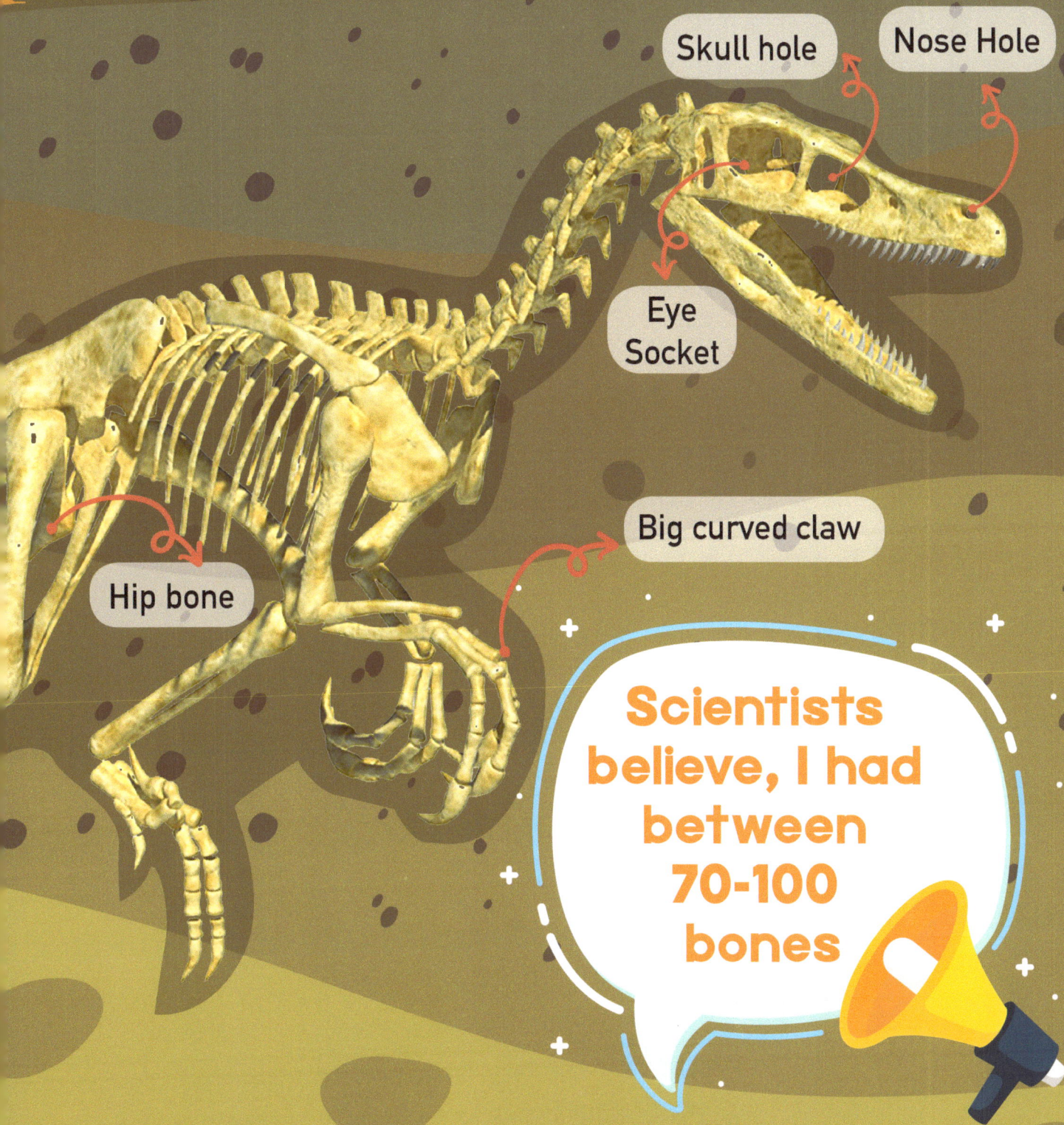

Large Velociraptor compared with a 1.8 meter tall person.

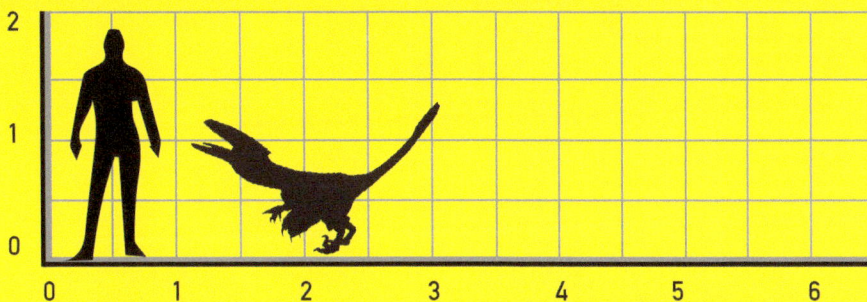

DILOPHOSAURUS

" TWO CRESTED LIZARD "

dy-loh-fo-sawr-us

This dinosaur had a couple of crests along the top of its head. The similarity with the cockerel crest indicates that their main function was visual communication with peers.

I AM ONE OF THE

Long thin legs

SEE ME IN REAL

When: 193 MYS   **Where:** North America   **Period:** Early Jurassic   **Habitat:** Rainforest and swamp

Two flattened semi-circular crests on the head.

GENUS DINOSAURS

S shape nack

Weak teeth at the back of the upper jaw and firm teeth at the front. This is why they may not have had the capability to kill large prey using their mouth

Short arms with 3 fingered clawed hand

Three-toed feet with sharp claws (plus a dewclaw)

Length: 7 m   **Height:** 1.8 m   **Weight:** 400 Kg   **Diet:** Small animals and fish

DILOPHOSAURUS
SKULL

Rounded
crests bones

Skull hole

Nose hole

12 maxillary teeth and as
many as 18 dentary teeth

Triassic Period	Jurassic Period	Cretaceous Period
251 Million Years Ago	200 Million Years Ago	145 Million Years Ago

Mesozoic Era

Eye socket

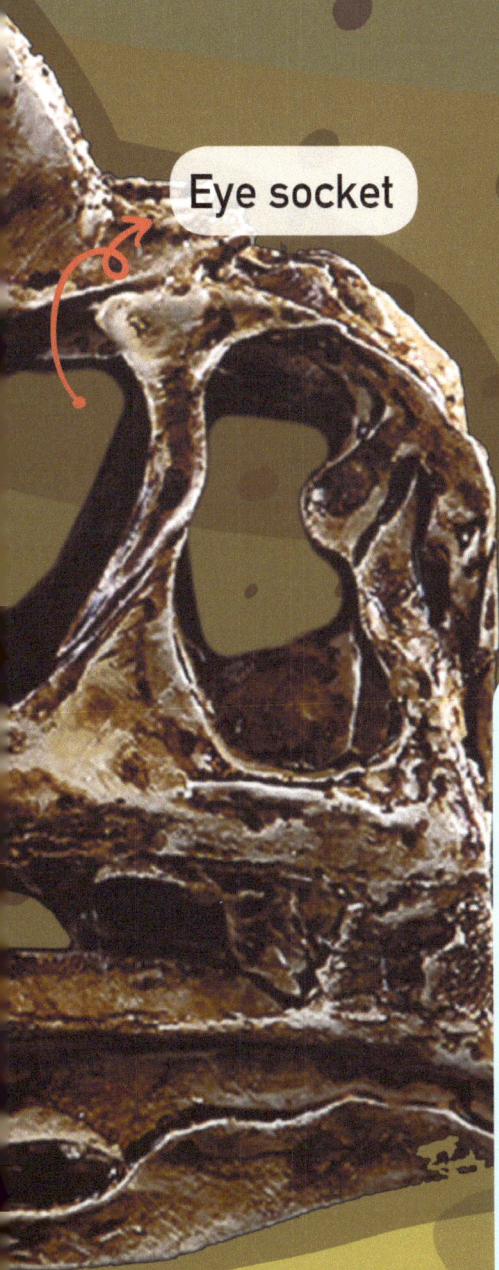

Scientists have found only 5 skeletons and all were found in Arizona

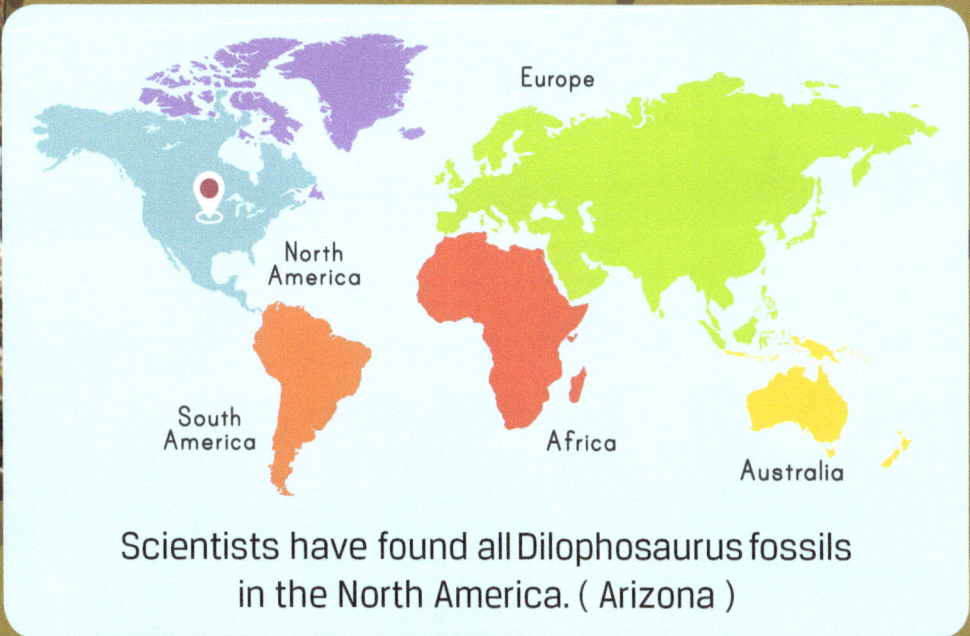

Europe

North America

South America

Africa

Australia

Scientists have found all Dilophosaurus fossils in the North America. (Arizona)

Large Dilophosaurus compared with a 1.8 meter tall person.

2

1

0

0 1 2 3 4 5 6

THEROPODS

" BEAST- FOOTED "

theh-ruh-podz

The T-Rex family (Theropod dinosaurs) ruled the planet for millions of years, with species ranging from the mighty Tyrannosaurus rex to feathered raptors no bigger than turkeys.

These dinosaurs are the only meat-eating group of dinosaurs. They walked on three-toed bird-like feet with sharp claws. They had powerful legs and short arms.

SHARP TEETH
Jagged teeth helped to pierce and rip meat.

THICK TAILS
A chunky tail helped meat-eaters keep their balance.

GOOD EYESIGHT
Forward-facing eyes gave carnivores excellent vision to spot prey.

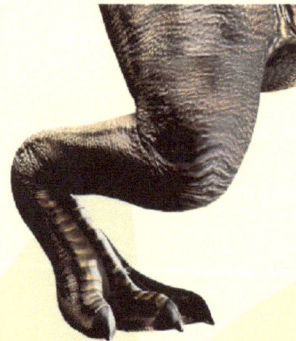

FAST LEGS
Strong legs helped hunters chase down speedy prey.

STRONG JAWS
Powerful jaws were ideal for grabbing prey and crushing their bones.

www.ingramcontent.com/pod-product-compliance
Lightning Source LLC
Chambersburg PA
CBHW060845270326
41933CB00003B/203

T-REX FAMILY

Theropod dinosaurs are the only meat-eating group of dinosaurs. They walked on three-toed bird-like feet with sharp claws They had powerful legs and short arms

ISBN 9780645481624

90000

9 780645 481624

Growing Self-Esteem through Yoga

Helping children reach their highest potential

TRUST

Happy CARE

KINDNESS Love

LIFE nurtu

Grace

RESPEC

PEACE

Loyalty

GENTLENESS

NATURE

Resilience

HOPE

Live Love Yoga

Fits into the Curriculum under PDHPE and Character Development

Monica Batiste